This book belongs to

_____

YOU ALWAYS HAVE
A FRIEND
IN JESUS
for Girls

ELIZABETH GEORGE

HARVEST HOUSE PUBLISHERS
EUGENE, OREGON

Cover by Dugan Design Group

Cover Images © kolesnikovserg / Fotolia; Monalyn Gracia / Alamy

YOU ALWAYS HAVE A FRIEND IN JESUS FOR GIRLS

Copyright © 2016 Elizabeth George
Published by Harvest House Publishers
Eugene, Oregon 97402
www.harvesthousepublishers.com

ISBN 978-0-7369-5523-2 (pbk.)
ISBN 978-0-7369-5524-9 (eBook)

Library of Congress Cataloging-in-Publication Data
Names: George, Elizabeth, 1944- author.
Title: You always have a friend in Jesus for girls / Elizabeth George.
Description: Eugene, Oregon : Harvest House Publishers, 2016.
Identifiers: LCCN 2015042037 | ISBN 9780736955232 (pbk.)
Subjects: LCSH: Jesus Christ—Textbooks. | Girls—Religious life—Textbooks.
Classification: LCC BT207 .G46 2016 | DDC 248.8/2—dc23 LC record available at
https://lccn.loc.gov/2015042037

Printed in the United States of America

16 17 18 19 20 21 22 23 24 / VP-JC / 10 9 8 7 6 5 4 3 2 1

Contents

1. Jesus Is Your Friend 7

2. Jesus Is a Friend Who Loves at All Times 17

3. Jesus Is a Friend You Can Trust 27

4. Jesus Is a Friend Who Prays for You 39

5. Jesus Is a Friend Who Shows You How to Serve . . . 51

6. Jesus Is a Friend Who Understands You 65

7. Jesus Is a Friend Who Is Gracious 79

8. Jesus Is a Friend Who Is Generous 91

9. Jesus Is a Friend Who Is Faithful 103

10. Jesus Is a Friend Who Is Wise 113

1

Jesus Is Your Friend

The only thing better than a friend...is a best friend. You know, someone you can spend hours and hours together with and never run out of things to talk about or exciting things to do. A best friend is someone you like, trust, count on, and spend as much time with as you possibly can—as much as your parents will allow.

But friendships are with people, and many times they let you down. Maybe they turn on you or turn away from you. Maybe they drop you cold as a friend. And sadly, maybe they move away.

But the good news is Jesus will *never* let you down. He is a friend forever. And Jesus will *never* turn on you or turn away from you, or drop you as His friend. And Jesus will *never* move away and leave you. Jesus is your forever friend.

You probably already know that Jesus is a very special person. That's an understatement, because He is the most special person who ever lived! That's why you won't read very far in the New Testament books of the Bible—especially Matthew, Mark, Luke, or John—before you discover that the stories of Jesus contain many life lessons and show you character qualities about Jesus and His relationship with people. He always treated people with kindness and helped and healed many who were sick. He even raised some people from the dead!

Jesus was also the greatest teacher who ever lived and the greatest person who ever lived. His life, death, and resurrection from the dead have transformed the lives of millions of people since He returned to heaven almost 2000 years ago.

Are you thinking, *Yes, I know Jesus is a special person, but what does this mean to me?* Well, to begin to answer this question, think about this: The greatest of all people who have ever lived—Jesus Christ—wants to get to know *you* and become *your* friend. Look at what happened to some of the people who followed Jesus—to them He said:

> *I no longer call you servants, because a servant does not know his master's business. Instead, I have called you friends, for everything that I learned from my Father I have made known to you* (John 15:15).

Can you think of some nice things that might happen if Jesus was your friend? List them here:

_____

_____

_____

Fun in God's Word!

It's always good to know the person who says he or she wants to be your friend. So let's take a few minutes and have some fun in God's Word as we get to know J-E-S-U-S.

Jesus is the Son of God. Many kids—and adults too—get confused when Jesus is called "the Son of God." They think this means that Jesus was not God, but was only God's Son, which makes them think that Jesus is someone less than God. But read the verse below and answer this question: How did these people respond when Jesus announced He was the Son of God?

For this reason [the Jews] tried all the more to kill him; not only was he breaking the Sabbath, but he was even calling God his own Father, making himself equal with God (John 5:18).

_____

_____

_____

According to John 20:31, what is the purpose of the Gospel of John, or the book of John?

These [things—the words and messages in the Gospel of John] are written that you may believe that Jesus is the Messiah, the Son of God.

_____

_____

According to the rest of John 20:31, what is the result of believing Jesus is the Son of God?

...that by believing you may have life in his name.

_____

_____

Thomas, one of the Jesus' disciples, heard Jesus say He was "the Son of God." He also heard others call Jesus by that title. What did Thomas call Jesus, knowing He was "the Son of God"?

Thomas answered and said to Him, "My Lord and my God!" (John 20:28 NASB).

_____

_____

Jesus is truly special because He is God who made heaven and earth. He created the first people on planet Earth, Adam and Eve. He had a special relationship with them. And now Jesus, who was God in human flesh, wants to be *your* friend. That's pretty cool, right? Actually, that's epic!

What else did Jesus do? Read on to discover that He...

Entered this world as a baby. God is Spirit, which means He does not have a body. Since the time everything was created, God has wanted to have a personal relationship with the people He has created. To make that possible, He had to became a man. Read the verses below and write out how God became a man.

You [Mary] will conceive and give birth to a son, and you are to call him Jesus (Luke 1:31).

Now look at the many exciting descriptions of what this "child" would become and accomplish.

— *He will be great and*

— *will be called the Son of the Most High.*

— *The Lord God will give him the throne of his father David, and*

— *he will reign over Jacob's descendants;*

— *his kingdom will never end* (Luke 1:32-33).

How does your impression and understanding of Jesus need to be corrected or changed, based on these descriptions of Jesus as God?

_____

_____

The angel promised Mary that a baby would be born. According to the verses below, where did the angel tell the shepherds they could find this very special baby?

Today in the town of David [Bethlehem] a Savior has been born to you; he is the Messiah, the Lord. This will be a sign to you: You will find a baby wrapped in cloths and lying in a manger (Luke 1:11-12).

_____

_____

Once Jesus was born, He was God in a human body. He was a human person, like you and me. But He was also God, and He possessed all of the qualities of God, which means Jesus possessed a perfect, sinless nature. He was and is 100 percent God and 100 percent man. Jesus also...

$\mathcal{S}$acrificed Himself for His friends. It takes a very special friend to be willing to die for another person. And yet that is what Jesus said He was willing to do for His friends and you. According to John 15:13, what is the proof of the greatest love in the world?

Greater love has no one than this: to lay down one's life for one's friends (John 15:13).

_____

_____

How did Jesus demonstrate His love for His friends—and you—according to Romans 5:8?

God demonstrates his own love for us in this: While we were still sinners, Christ died for us.

_____

_____

nites His friends with God's heavenly family. Jesus wants to be your friend, but with that friendship comes an additional relationship. What does God the Father want to do through your friendship with His Son?

God decided in advance to adopt us into his own family by bringing us to himself through Jesus Christ. This is what he wanted to do, and it gave him great pleasure (Ephesians 1:5 NLT).

_____

_____

When you come into God's family through your friendship with Jesus, what gift does the Father give to you, according to Galatians 4:6 (NLT)?

Because we are his children, God has sent the Spirit of his Son into our hearts, prompting us to call out, "Abba, Father."

_____

_____

_____

What an awesome truth—When Jesus becomes your friend, He comes to live in your heart!

$\int$ecures eternal life for His friends. Jesus offers His friends a special kind of life—eternal life. *Eternal* means lasting forever. It means having no end. What do you need to do to receive eternal life, to receive this life that has no ending?

God so loved the world that he gave his one and only Son, that whoever believes in him [Jesus] shall not perish but have eternal life (John 3:16).

_____

_____

_____

Do you believe that Jesus is God and that He died for your sins? If so, God the Father wants you as a friend for His Son!

What a Friend You Have in Jesus!

Throughout this book you will read many stories from Jesus' life that are found in the Bible. They will help you understand that God came to this earth as a man so He could provide an opportunity for you to be His friend. Each chapter you read will show you how superspecial it is to be God's friend through His Son, Jesus.

Jesus Is Your Friend

In this chapter we had some fun in God's Word learning that J-E-S-U-S is God, and J-E-S-U-S wants to have a personal relationship with you and be your friend. Think about how special your friend J-E-S-U-S is as you write out the points for each letter. (I'll get you started with "J.")

J esus is the Son of God and He...

E _____

S _____

U _____

S _____

Write out one thing you liked, learned, or want to do after discovering that Jesus wants to be your forever friend.

_____

_____

_____

A Prayer to Pray

Jesus, it's hard to make a friend and to be a friend. Thank You for wanting to be my friend. I'm so glad that I can receive You into my heart and be Your friend even before we meet in heaven. Amen.

2

Jesus Is a Friend Who Loves at All Times

It's easy to love friends who love you back. Friendships are also easy to keep when you don't ask very much from your friends. But what about times when you really need their help? Are they still there when you ask for their help? And what if that help is needed for a while, even a long while? The mark of a true friend is long-lasting love.

People tend to define *love* as some sort of physical attraction, but the Bible has another way of looking at love and measuring it. And best of all, the Bible shows the perfect person to demonstrate God's definition of love—Jesus Christ.

Fun in God's Word!

Because Jesus is the perfect example of love, He is the very first person you want to look at and learn from when it comes to love. Jesus loved God, the Father. Jesus loved His family. He loved His disciples. He loved the people who followed Him. He loved those who were sad, hungry, suffering, sick, and dying. And He loves you! Jesus also instructed you and all His people to *"love one another"* (John 13:34). Let's see how Jesus showed His love so you can be more like Him and love the people in your life.

Jesus loved His friends. Can you imagine having Jesus in your very own home when you have a need? That's what happened in John 11, when Jesus' friend Lazarus became sick and died. You can probably guess how miserable Lazarus's two sisters must have been! You can read the complete story of Jesus' visit to their home in John 11, but for now read John 11:5 below. What does it say about Jesus' feelings toward Lazarus, Martha, and Mary—His three friends?

Now Jesus loved Martha and her sister and Lazarus.

_____

_____

Can you think of a time when you came to the aid of a friend who was suffering? What did you do?

_____

_____

There are lots of things you can do when a friend is going through a difficult time. You may need your parents' help, but you can make a card. You can write out a prayer. You can call her. You can gather up a few of your favorite things—craft items, special markers, stickers, or pens—and leave them at her house. What will you do the next time a friend of yours is in need?

_____

_____

Jesus loved His fellow workers. One of Jesus' fellow workers was John. What does this verse tell you about Jesus' relationship with His disciple John?

One of them, the disciple whom Jesus loved [John], was reclining next to him (John 13:23).

_____

What does this verse tell you about Jesus' feelings toward all of His disciples?

It was just before the Passover Festival. Jesus knew that the hour had come for him to leave this world and go to the

Father. Having loved his own who were in the world, he loved them to the end (John 13:1).

_____

_____

It's easy to love your family and friends, but what about other kids at school? Jesus wants you to love them too. Is there a girl at school who is new or doesn't seem to have a friend? List a few things you could do to reach out to her and show Jesus' kind of love. And check with your mom. She will probably have some great ideas!

_____

_____

_____

Jesus loved His enemies. Oh my—here's a hard one! Again, it's easy to love your family and friends, but it's really hard to love those kids who give you a hard time. Maybe there are some mean girls at school or in your neighborhood. Maybe there's a group that won't let you in—maybe they even make fun of you. In Matthew 5:44, what did Jesus say you are to do?

I tell you, love your enemies and pray for those who perse-cute you.

_____

_____

How did Jesus respond to the people who nailed Him on the cross?

Father, forgive them, for they do not know what they are doing (Luke 23:34).

_____

_____

Most kids aren't really mean, and they are not really the "enemy." Many times they don't know how to act or they feel awkward, so they lash out. Whatever you do, don't treat them the way they treat you! What does Jesus tell you to do instead?

Do to others as you would have them do to you (Luke 6:31).

_____

_____

Follow Jesus' advice and treat other kids the way you want them to treat you. Then see what happens!

Jesus loved you enough to die for you. What did Jesus do to show us what love is?

This is how we know what love is: Jesus Christ laid down his life for us (1 John 3:16).

_____

_____

God is love, and He showed us what love is by sending His only Son, Jesus, to earth. How else did Jesus show us His love?

God demonstrates his own love for us in this: While we were still sinners, Christ died for us (Romans 5:8).

_____

_____

Read John 1:12 (NASB) below. What should be your response to the fact that Jesus loved you so much that He died to save you from your sins?

As many as received Him, to them He gave the right to become children of God, to those who believe in His name.

_____

_____

_____

A question for your heart: Have you believed in Jesus Christ and received Him as your Savior and friend?

What a Friend You Have in Jesus!

When you feel all alone or think that no one understands you or likes you, remember Jesus. He is your friend when no one else is. He is your friend today and forever.

There is never a minute—or even a second—that He is not with you, loving you, encouraging you, and comforting you. And that's the kind of love He wants you to give to others. Here's how your friend Jesus wants you to love: Circle the word *love* every time it is used in these verses:

Love—chooses God as Number One in importance. "'*You shall love the* LORD *your God with all your heart, with all your soul, and with all your mind.' This is the first and great commandment*" (Matthew 22:37-38 NKJV).

Love—chooses others as the next priority. "*The second is like it: 'You shall love your neighbor as yourself'*" (verse 39 NKJV).

Love—chooses to obey Jesus. "*If you love Me, keep My commandments*" (John 14:15 NKJV).

Love—chooses to follow Jesus' command to love others. "*A new commandment I give to you, that you love one another; as I have loved you, that you also love one another*" (John 13:34 NKJV).

Love—chooses to forgive rather than seek revenge. "*Love your enemies, bless those who curse you, do good to those who hate you, and pray for those who spitefully use you and persecute you*" (Matthew 5:43-44 NKJV).

Jesus Is a Friend Who Loves at All Times

In this chapter we have had some fun in God's Word. Look back at the four facts about Jesus' love for others and write out the points that show you how Jesus loved others—including you!

Jesus loved His friends

$\mathcal{J}$ _____

$\mathcal{J}$ _____

$\mathcal{J}$ _____

Write out one thing you liked, learned, or want to do now after discovering that Jesus is a friend who loves at all times.

_____

_____

_____

_____

_____

A Prayer to Pray

Jesus, I love learning more about You—especially about how much You love me. Now will You please help me to love the people in my life at home, at school, at church, and everywhere else I go? I need it! Amen.

3

Jesus Is a Friend You Can Trust

As a girl and a young woman you have probably been hurt, disappointed, or let down by a friend or someone else you trusted. Maybe you trusted them with some very personal and private information...and your friend shared it with someone else. Or you thought someone was one of your best-of-the-best friends...and suddenly one day you discovered that another girl had taken your "best friend" place and you were left out.

When friendships are broken or someone turns on you, it's easy to stop trusting all people. The pain of an ended friendship can last a long time. But here's some good news for you: You can always, *always* trust Jesus! He is a friend you can definitely and totally trust 100 percent of the time, every day, and in every way. In fact, Jesus promises, *"Surely I am with you always, to the very end of the age"* (Matthew 28:20).

While Jesus walked on this earth He was a close friend to His 12 disciples. But as He began to move toward His death on the cross, His disciples became extremely nervous that He—their best friend—was leaving them. Jesus had chosen them to be His friends, taught them, mentored them, prayed with them and for them, and protected them. In His prayer on the night before Judas betrayed Him, Jesus prayed these words to His Father in heaven:

While I was with them [the disciples], I protected them... None has been lost except the one doomed to destruction so that Scripture would be fulfilled (John 17:12).

How many of His friends did Jesus lose?

_____

Who was the exception, and why?

_____

_____

Even though there were times when the disciples did not understand what Jesus was saying, and even though at times they questioned and doubted, the disciples knew this one thing: They could trust Jesus.

Fun in God's Word!

The disciples knew they could trust Jesus, and now it's time for you to realize that Jesus is a friend *you* can T-R-U-S-T.

*T*rust Jesus with your salvation. The disciples were kept under Jesus' protection while He was with them, and He lost none of them except Judas, who willfully betrayed Jesus. Like the disciples, you can fully trust Jesus and depend on Him for all things, including your eternal life. Write out the three promises Jesus gave to His friends in John 10:28.

I give them eternal life,
and they shall never perish;
no one will snatch them out of my hand.

Promise #1 _____

_____

Promise #2 _____

_____

Promise #3 _____

_____

According to John 10:29, who else is involved in making certain of your salvation besides Jesus, and what did He promise?

My Father, who has given them [the disciples and Jesus' friends] to me, is greater than all; no one can snatch them out of my Father's hand.

_____

_____

Remember Jesus gives you a helper. Jesus knew His friends would have a hard time after He returned to heaven. During His time with them on earth He kept them safe, and they relied on Him to lead them. So to support them in the future, after He left earth, Jesus promised to send "a helper" who would take His place. Circle the words in these verses that describe what this special "helper" does for you as one of Jesus' friends and followers:

> *I will ask the Father, and he will give you another advocate [or counselor] to help you and be with you forever—the Spirit of truth. The world cannot accept him, because it neither sees him nor knows him. But you know him, for he lives with you and will be in you* (John 14:16-17).

The disciples trusted that Jesus would keep His promise to send a Helper, a Counselor, the Spirit of truth. And sure enough, Jesus kept His promise! In Acts 2:1-4, we learn that the Father sent the Holy Spirit to live in Jesus' friends, and also in all those who trust in Him to help them. Jesus also...

Understands your struggles. Do you ever feel like nobody understands your problems or what you are going through? Even your parents don't always understand. But your friend Jesus knows all about every single one of your problems. He understands your struggles.

We do not have a high priest [Jesus] who is unable to empathize with our weaknesses, but we have one who has been tempted in every way, just as we are—yet he did not sin (Hebrews 4:15).

Why is Jesus able to understand and help you with your problems?

_____

_____

_____

According to Mark 1:13, how long did Jesus struggle with temptation when He began His ministry?

He was in the wilderness forty days, being tempted by Satan (Mark 1:13).

_____

_____

When you face a struggle and are tempted to give up, remember that you can trust Jesus because He too was tempted. He knows exactly what you are going through! He has "been there and done that." And because He knows your struggles, you can talk to Him in prayer about them. Jesus *"did not sin,"* which means He can help you deal with your temptations and keep you from making a wrong decision.

$\mathcal{S}$peaks only the truth. Jesus was and is the truth—and spoke only the truth. What three things does Jesus say about Himself in John 14:6?

Jesus answered, "I am the way and the truth and the life. No one comes to the Father except through me."

Description #1 _____

Description #2 _____

Description #3 _____

Why is it important to have a personal relationship with Jesus, according to the last part of John 14:6?

_____

_____

Read John 8:44. This verse was spoken to a group of "religious" leaders. Underline the bad qualities and actions that describe the devil:

You belong to your father, the devil...He was a murderer from the beginning, not holding to the truth, for there is no truth in him. When he lies, he speaks his native language, for he is a liar and the father of lies.

List how the devil is described when it comes to telling the truth:

_____

_____

Jesus is "the truth" (John 14:6), and He wants you as His friend and follower to also tell the truth. What do these verses say you should always do?

Each of you must put off falsehood and speak truthfully to your neighbor (Ephesians 4:25).

_____

_____

[Be] speaking the truth in love (Ephesians 4:15).

_____

Jesus makes it very clear that lying has no place in the lives of His friends and followers. To believe in Jesus—who is the truth and spoke the truth—means you, too, are to speak only the truth. Do you wish to please God and live—and speak—as His Son did? Then focus on living out this verse:

The LORD detests lying lips, but he delights in people who are trustworthy (Proverbs 12:22).

Thank Jesus for being trustworthy. Do you have a friend who is completely honest with you all the time? If you do, you have a rare friend indeed! Be thankful for her. And be thankful for Jesus, who can be trusted when He says something in His Word, the Bible. What does this verse say about Jesus' truthfulness?

The law was given through Moses; grace and truth came through Jesus Christ (John 1:17).

_____

_____

Jesus is someone you can trust because when He speaks, He speaks the truth. Always.

What a Friend You Have in Jesus!

Knowing that Jesus loves you and wants to be your friend should help you trust Jesus. He has promised to protect you. Here's a question for you: Because you can T-R-U-S-T Jesus, what response should you give back to Him? The answer? *Your trust.* Use T-R-U-S-T from Proverbs 3:5-6 to guide your response.

> *Trust in the LORD with all you heart*
> *and do not lean on your own understanding.*
> *In all your ways acknowledge Him,*
> *and He will make your paths straight* (NASB).

Trust in the Lord—"Trust in the LORD with all your heart." God knows 100 percent of the time what is 100 percent best for you. He is the 100-percent-best person to trust with every decision you need to make.

Refuse to trust in your own understanding—"...and do not lean on your own understanding." Do you know everything there is to know in the world? Nobody does. So rather than trying to do things by yourself with limited knowledge and understanding, lean on God's wisdom from His Word, the Bible. That's where God has written everything you need to know. And don't forget to ask your parents for help. They can provide wisdom too!

Understand and count on His presence—"In all your ways acknowledge Him." Jesus is always with you, even though you can't see Him. When you pray, you acknowledge Jesus and His presence and can talk to Him about every decision you must make and every problem you have. How great is that? Jesus is always there by your side—at all times, day or night.

Straight paths come with God's help—"...and He will make your paths straight." God's job is to direct and guide you through life along a straight and right path. If you trust Him, He will make clear the way you should travel. He will show you the decisions you should make. Then you can move forward in the right direction and do what is best for you and what pleases Him.

Take time to make your choices—Hopefully you have already chosen to trust Jesus with your salvation. Jesus is the Son of God and 100 percent holy and sinless. These facts about God present a big problem because 100 percent of all people in the world are sinful. As a result, 100 percent of all people are separated from God. (That's the bad news.) But the good news is that because of Jesus' death on the cross, you can accept by faith that Jesus died in your place for your sins. Because of Jesus, you can have forgiveness for your sins.

According to Ephesians 1:7, two things happen when you put your faith and trust in Jesus. What are they?

In him [Jesus] we have redemption through his blood, the forgiveness of sins, in accordance with the riches of God's grace.

Happening #1 _____

_____

Happening #2 _____

_____

Jesus Is a Friend You Can Trust

In this chapter we had some fun in God's Word as we learned that we can **T-R-U-S-T** Jesus. On this page, write out the point for each letter. (I'll get you started with "T.")

Trust Jesus with your salvation

R_____

U_____

S_____

T_____

Write out one thing you liked, learned, or want to do now that you know you can trust your friend Jesus in every area of your life.

_____

_____

_____

_____

_____

A Prayer to Pray

Thank You, Jesus, for being the best friend I could ever have. Help me to trust You with all my heart. I *really* need Your help to make better decisions every day. I'm so glad You are my friend and will show me the right path. Amen.

4

Jesus Is a Friend Who Prays for You

It's impossible to read about the life of Jesus in the Gospels—in Matthew, Mark, Luke, and John—and not notice that He prayed a L-O-T. For Jesus, praying was like breathing. It was as if He couldn't live without praying. His one desire was to do what God, the Father, wanted Him to do. In His last recorded prayer to the Father before He went to the cross, Jesus said, *"I have brought you glory on earth by finishing the work you gave me to do"* (John 17:4).

How was Jesus able to finish His work on earth? Prayer was a major tool He used for completing everything He was asked to do by the Father. Would you like to have this ability to do everything God wants you to do? Well, prayer—as modeled by Jesus—is a big step toward knowing what you need to do.

Fun in God's Word!

You can never know enough about Jesus! Hopefully you have received Him as your Savior—if so, then He is your friend. He is the Son of God, and the Son of Man. He was born in a stable, yet His reign is in heaven. On and on go the wonders of our wonderful Jesus. Jesus also held, and still holds, three positions in the universe—He was a Prophet, He is a Priest, and He will be a King.

Right now let's look at Jesus' role as a Priest, like that of the Old Testament priests. One of the functions of a priest was to pray for the people of Israel, which is what Jesus did too. He prayed for His friends in the same way the Old Testament priests prayed for God's people. Here are some facts about Jesus' prayers:

Jesus' prayers are continuous. Jesus spent His earthly ministry helping people and praying for them. After He was raised from the dead, He returned to heaven. What is Jesus doing in heaven right now for His friends—for *"those who come to God through him"*—as seen in Hebrews 7:25?

He is able to save completely those who come to God through him, because he always lives to intercede [pray] for them.

_____

_____

Think about it—Jesus is in heaven continually praying for you all the time! That's what a friend does, and Jesus is concerned about His friends, including you. Your friends at school or at church or on your ball team—or even next door—and your parents and pesky brother and sister are people Jesus wants you to be praying for here on earth. Write down the names of the girls who are your best friends, the ones you spend the most time with.

_____

_____

_____

Jot down a few things you can pray for these friends, and begin to be a friend who prays.

_____

_____

_____

Jesus' prayers have authority. A person who has authority is a person who has the ability to make things happen. Your parents have authority, and so do your teachers and those who are government officials. And guess what? Jesus has the greatest of all authority. When Jesus, as God the Son, returned to heaven, He sat down at the Father's "right hand," which is a position of power and authority. What does the Bible say Jesus is doing while He sits on His throne of authority?

There is one God and one mediator between God and mankind, the man Christ Jesus (1 Timothy 2:5).

_____

_____

A mediator is someone who helps explain to one person what is going on in another person's life. This is exactly what Jesus is doing for you. With His authority as God's Son, Jesus is explaining to the Father that you are His friend and that He—Jesus—is personally helping you do the right things in your life.

Because you are a friend of Jesus, you have authority too.

Jesus' prayers are for God's will. Read the following prayers from Jesus. What were some of the occasions for His prayers, according to these verses?

Jesus went out to a mountainside to pray, and spent the night praying to God. When morning came, he called his disciples to him and chose twelve of them (Luke 6:12-13).

Here you see Jesus praying for God's will regarding...

_____

_____

_____

Simon, Simon, Satan has asked to sift all of you as wheat. But I have prayed for you, Simon, that your faith may not fail (Luke 22:31-32).

Here you read Jesus' prayer for God's will that...

_____

_____

_____

Jesus was praying right before He was betrayed

...He went away a second time and prayed, "My Father, if it is not possible for this cup [of death] to be taken away unless I drink it, may your will be done" (Matthew 26:42).

Here you witness Jesus praying for God's will regarding...

_____

_____

Jesus did not want to do anything the Father did not want Him to do. He wanted to do God's will. He prayed before choosing the disciples. He prayed that Simon Peter's faith would remain strong. And He prayed just before going to the cross for God's will to be done.

Jesus also told His disciples to make sure their prayers lined up with the Father's desires. He even taught them how to pray, and what to pray for. He said:

Pray like this:

Our Father in heaven,
  may your name be kept holy.
May your Kingdom come soon.
May your will be done on earth,
  as it is in heaven (Matthew 6:9-10 NLT).

Underline the last sentence of Jesus' instructions about how to pray. Knowing "God's will" means you know what the Father wants you to make decisions and live your life.

What a Friend You Have in Jesus!

Jesus spent much of His life on earth praying for His friends. He also prayed for the Father to lead Him in doing what was necessary to ensure salvation for His friends. Today Jesus is in heaven praying for you at all times. His life of prayer shows you how you too can be praying for others.

But lots of kids (and even adults) have this problem: They don't feel like they know how to pray. Maybe you've had this happen to you. You are with other kids at church and the teacher asks if anyone wants to pray. You would like to pray, but you are not sure what to say. Or maybe because you don't know how to pray, you are hoping like crazy that the teacher won't ask you to pray.

Well, you are not alone. Jesus' disciples had this very same problem. They heard Jesus' prayers and watched Him pray to the Father. Finally they asked Jesus, *"Lord, teach us to pray"* (Luke 11:1). Here is a model prayer Jesus then gave to His disciples, which is also given to you as a guide for your own prayers.

> *Father, may your name be kept holy.*
>   *May your Kingdom come soon.*
> *Give us each day the food we need,*
> *and forgive us our sins,*
>   *as we forgive those who sin against us.*
> *And don't let us yield to temptation* (Luke 11:2-4 NLT).

So now you have a guide on how to pray. But maybe you still don't quite understand how prayer works. Using the acrostic **P-R-A-Y** will help you to become more confident as you pray for yourself, your family, and your friends.

Prayer is talking to God. You probably don't have a problem talking to your parents or your friends. In fact, you could talk with your friends for hours! Well, it's the same when you talk to God. Read on to see what this verse says you need to do to get closer to God.

Draw near to God with a sincere heart (Hebrews 10:22).

What is it you are to do? _____

_____

What attitude should you have in your heart when you pray?

_____

Learning to talk to God is just like making friends. To make a friend, you need to take the first step and start talking to him or her. It's the same way with God. Take the first step and say, "Hello, God, my name is _____. I want to be Your friend, and I have a few things I need to talk over with You." When you talk to God, be respectful and be yourself—be sincere. God wants you to just be yourself—the real you—when you talk to Him.

Remember you must pray with a heart of faith. God has promised to answer your prayers, so you must believe that He will keep this promise. That's faith! Here's how you should pray:

Whatever you ask for in prayer, believe that you have received it, and it will be yours (Mark 11:24).

What is your job or part in prayer?

_____ and _____

What does the verse above say happens as a result of your asking with a heart of faith?

_____

Does this mean that you can ask and get anything you want, like a new bike or a video game? For help with the answer, look at the verse below. What are you not to do when you pray?

When you ask, you do not receive, because you ask with wrong motives, that you may spend what you get on your pleasures (James 4:3).

_____

_____

_____

Ask, knowing that God promises to hear your prayers. Often we don't understand how God works. For instance, the God of the universe wants us to be a part of what He is doing in and around us—even though we don't know why. So when God promises us that He hears and answers our prayers, we need to believe Him and start praying. Notice and underline what God is promising to you when you **A-S-K**:

Ask and it will be given to you;

Seek and you will find;

Knock and the door will be opened to you (Matthew 7:7).

In the verse that follows, circle what you are to do and underline what God will do:

Call to me and I will answer you and tell you great and unsearchable things you do not know (Jeremiah 33:3).

You need to confess sin before you pray. A big reason kids don't pray is because they have done something wrong and won't admit it. It's like not looking your parents in the eye because you know you did something you weren't supposed to do. (For instance, lying to them!) So, like with your parents, you need to admit the truth to God and tell Him you are sorry for what you did. You need to agree with God that it was wrong. Take a look at a few verses that talk about confessing your sin.

If I regard [sin] in my heart, the Lord will not hear (Psalm 66:18 NKJV).

What happens to your prayers when you sin and don't confess them to God?

_____

If we confess our sins, he is faithful and just and will forgive us our sins and purify us from all unrighteousness (1 John 1:9).

What happens when you do confess your sin and admit it to God?

_____

_____

_____

Could you have any better friend than Jesus? Of course not. First, Jesus is always praying for you, day and night—when you are awake, and when you are sleeping. Second, as you have seen in this chapter, your friend Jesus has given you a way to learn how to pray for yourself and others. Truly, Jesus is the greatest friend you can have!

Jesus Is a Friend Who Prays for You

In this chapter we had some fun in God's Word as we learned how your friend Jesus prays for you. But just as important, we have also learned what it means to **P-R-A-Y**. On this page, write out the points that talk about what it means when you **P-R-A-Y**. (I'll get you started with "P.")

Prayer is talking to God

R _____

A _____

Y _____

Write out one thing you liked, learned, or want to do now after discovering that Jesus is a friend who prays for you all the time.

_____

_____

_____

_____

A Prayer to Pray

Lord Jesus, I'm so glad You are a true friend I can talk to. I'm so glad You are there and You promise to really listen to me when I pray. Thank You for being my forever friend. Amen.

5

Jesus Is a Friend Who Shows You How to Serve

Most people all around the world, Christians and non-Christians, past and present, agree Jesus was a great person. Are you wondering, *What did Jesus do that has caused people around the globe to acknowledge Him as the greatest man of all times, the greatest man who ever lived?* Well, here's what Jesus *didn't* do. As a man, He...

never wrote a book.

never commanded an army of soldiers or won great battles in war.

never encouraged people to revolt.

Now here's what Jesus *did* do. The powerful quality in His life that made Him stand out above all others who ever lived was, in a very few words, *He served others*. Jesus was aware of the needs of others, and He was ready to help meet those needs, whether they were physical or spiritual.

And today? Jesus is still meeting the needs of His friends, as these verses declare:

...because Jesus lives forever, he has a permanent priesthood. Therefore he is able to save completely those who come to God through him, because he always lives to intercede for them. Such a high priest truly meets our need—one who is holy, blameless, pure, set apart from sinners, exalted above the heavens (Hebrews 7:24-26).

Fun in God's Word!

The first time that Jesus, God's Son and the Savior of the world, came to earth, it was as a lowly servant. What did He do to help others? Who were the people He served? What was His attitude? Look now to see how **S-E-R-V-I-C-E** was modeled by Jesus.

*S*erving describes Jesus' ministry on earth. Read the two prophecies below that tell us about the first time Jesus came to earth. Circle what the prophets called Jesus, the coming Messiah and the Savior of the world.

Here is my servant, whom I uphold, my chosen one in whom I delight (Isaiah 42:1).

See, my servant will act wisely; he will be raised and lifted up and highly exalted (Isaiah 52:13).

valuate whom you are serving. Very early in His ministry, Jesus was *"tempted by the devil"* (Matthew 4:1). Can you imagine what it must have been like for Jesus to be tempted and tested for 40 days and 40 nights? During that time, He went without food. The devil promised Jesus three things—food, power, and glory—if He would fall down and worship and serve the devil. Underline what Jesus said in response to the devil (or Satan, as he is also called)?

> *Jesus said to him, "Away from me, Satan! For it is written: 'Worship the Lord your God, and serve him only'"* (Matthew 4:10).

Jesus would not serve anyone but God the Father, and He also wants you to do the same—to worship and serve no one but the Father. Read Colossians 3:23-24 (NKJV) and answer a few questions about serving others.

> *And whatever you do, do it heartily, as to the Lord and not to men, knowing that from the Lord you will receive the reward of the inheritance; for you serve the Lord Christ.*

When you serve, what should your attitude be?

_____

Whom are you really serving when you serve others?

_____

Remember the variety of ways you can serve God and His people. The Bible is filled with stories about men and women—even young girls like you!—whom God used in a mighty way. Let's look at some of these young women and see how God used them and their service to others.

Miriam was about age 12 when we meet her in Exodus 2:1-9. When the ruler of Egypt ordered that all the male Hebrew babies under age two were to be killed, Moses' mother placed baby Moses in a basket *and put it among the reeds along the bank of the Nile. His sister [Miriam] stood at a distance to see what would happen to him"* (verses 3-4). After Pharaoh's daughter found Moses, Miriam boldly approached and *"asked Pharaoh's daughter, 'Shall I go and get one of the Hebrew women to nurse the baby for you?'"* (verse 7). The result? *"Pharaoh's daughter said to her [Moses' mother], 'Take this baby and nurse him for me, and I will pay you'"* (verse 9).

What did Miriam do that served God's purposes and benefited His people?

_____

_____

_____

What can you do to be more like Miriam?

_____

_____

_____

In 2 Kings 5, you can read the story of a young servant girl who served the wife of Naaman, the commander of the army of a pagan king. Naaman had leprosy. One day this girl, who was just like you, spoke up and *"said to her mistress, 'If only my master would see the prophet who is in Samaria! He would cure him of his leprosy'"* (verse 3). The result? Naaman went to the prophet Elisha's house, did as Elisha *"had told him, and his flesh was restored and became clean like that of a young boy"* (verse 14). Because this girl spoke of God, God was glorified when Namaan said, *"Now I know that there is no God in all the world except in Israel"* (verse 15).

What did the young servant girl do that served God's purposes and benefited His people?

_____

_____

_____

What can you do to be more like this young girl?

_____

_____

_____

The book of Esther features a young Jewish woman who was taken from her home and crowned queen under the pagan King Ahasuerus. She served God and His people by boldly going before the king to beg for her people—the Jews—to be saved from annihilation, saying, *"If it pleases* you, grant me my life—this is my petition. And spare my people—this is my request" (Esther 7:3). The result? The king "granted the Jews...the right to assemble and protect themselves" against all of their enemies (Esther 8:11).

What did Esther do that served God's purposes and benefited His people?

_____

_____

_____

What can you do to be more like Esther?

_____

_____

_____

Would you like to be used by God in some special way? All you have to do is desire to be "a servant" of His. What would this mean? *A servant is a person who is devoted to or guided by someone or something.* When your heart is "devoted to" and "guided by" God, you are on the right track to being a servant for real.

View serving God as your purpose in life. Serving God is not easy. Jesus was tempted to serve Satan instead of God. Yet throughout His earthly life and ministry, Jesus kept His focus on the Father's will and purpose for His life. Jesus wants you to have that same focus. You would never knowingly want to serve Satan, but sometimes you can slip and focus on other things instead of God's will. For instance, in Jesus' day, the religious leaders loved their worldly possessions, their things, their stuff. One day as they were listening to Jesus tell a story about a good servant (Luke 16:1-12), Jesus ended His story with this truth:

No one can serve two masters. Either you will hate the one and love the other, or you will be devoted to the one and despise the other. You cannot serve both God and money (Luke 16:13).

The point of Jesus' story is that you (and everyone else!) need to be careful not to choose to serve something or someone (including yourself!) other than God. For instance...

— Choosing to sleep a little longer, instead of getting up to read your Bible

— Choosing to talk or draw pictures or pass notes in church instead of listening to the Bible lesson

— Choosing to spend all of your allowance on yourself and not give any at church

Can you think of choices you can make that would help you to keep your focus on Jesus? Write out one or two here:

_____

_____

_____

Imagine what serving others looks like. It's often said, "One picture is worth a thousand words." Well, in the Bible, John 13 gives a very clear picture of what serving others looks like. Here is a part of that picture. Describe below what Jesus did as He was approaching His death:

He got up from the meal, took off his outer clothing, and wrapped a towel around his waist. After that, he poured water into a basin and began to wash his disciples' feet, drying them with the towel that was wrapped around him (John 13:4-5).

_____

_____

_____

Normally in a dry and dusty land like Judea, a servant would wash the dust and dirt off the feet of the people who arrived for supper. But on this occasion, there were no servants present, and none of Jesus' disciples wanted to act like a servant and perform the lowly task of washing the dirty feet of others. So Jesus did what His disciples were not willing to do. Can you think of a time when you have acted like a brat and chose not to be helpful when you could have acted like Jesus and helped out Mom or Dad or your brother or sister at home—when you could have served?

_____

_____

What will you do the next time you have an opportunity to serve?

_____

_____

Consider who Jesus wants you to serve. In the next verse, circle the "who" Jesus wants you to serve.

You, my brothers and sisters, were called to be free. But do not use your freedom to indulge the flesh; rather, serve one another humbly in love (Galatians 5:13).

Sometimes it's hard to get excited about serving other people. But here's something that will help you get excited about this: When you serve, who is it the Bible says you are really serving? Circle your answer.

Serve wholeheartedly, as if you were serving the Lord, not people (Ephesians 6:7).

Examine how you are serving. When you serve, Jesus values the *attitude* you have toward serving just as much as your *acts* of service. Note the two kinds of servants described in these two verses.

His master replied, "Well done, good and faithful servant! You have been faithful with a few things; I will put you in

charge of many things. Come and share your master's hap-
piness!" (Matthew 25:23).

His master replied, "You wicked, lazy servant! So you knew
that I harvest where I have not sown and gather where I
have not scattered seed?" (Matthew 25:26).

Both of these people were servants. But the wicked servant was called *"lazy"* and the faithful servant was called
"good." What does this tell you about how you should be
serving God and others?

Read the two verses above under the letter *C*—Galatians
5:13 and Ephesians 6:7—and write out what each verse
says about your attitude, about *how* you are to serve others.

Read Philippians 2:3-4 on the next page, and notice
what the verses say about the attitude you are to have while
serving others—both positive and negative.

3*Do nothing out of selfish ambition or vain conceit. Rather, in humility value others above yourselves,* 4*not looking to your own interests but each of you to the interests of the others.*

Wrong attitudes (verse 3) _____

_____

Right attitude (verse 3) _____

_____

Wrong attitude (verse 4) _____

_____

Right attitude (verse 4) _____

_____

What one change in your attitude could—or should— you make today?

_____

What a Friend You Have in Jesus!

Every day you are faced with dozens of opportunities to serve others. For example, someone accidentally spills out the contents of their backpack. Another person falls down and is hurt. Truthfully, you don't always feel like stopping to assist someone or rushing in and helping others. It takes time to serve people—and effort. And sometimes it is a risk because there are some people who make fun of you for caring, for getting involved, for getting your hands dirty as you help another student, or your brother or sister, wipe up a tumbled drink.

Are you struggling with the idea of even wanting to serve? If so, start by deciding you will do something whenever you see a need or see something that needs to be done. This can start with simply stopping and asking, "Do you need some help?" Decide you won't wait to see if someone else will do it (like the disciples did). Make it a personal goal to volunteer to serve at home, at school, and in your youth class at church. Open your heart, open your eyes, open your hands—and serve.

Most of all, look to Jesus. He came to earth with a different lifestyle and a radical message of humility and service. Jesus defined true greatness as serving others, and then He lived out that definition. Jesus' mission was to serve others and to give His life away—to die—for others. And that's exactly what He did.

Because Jesus is your friend and you are His friend, Jesus is asking and expecting you to follow His example—to be like Him, to join Him in serving others. He wants you to develop a servant's heart and help others by taking care of their needs just as He is taking care of you.

Jesus Is a Friend Who Shows You How to Serve

In this chapter we had some fun in God's Word as we learned that Jesus, the Son of God, was a servant the entire time He was on earth. We are to follow His example. We also spelled out S-E-R-V-I-C-E to help us understand what it means to serve. On this page, write out the point for each letter. (I'll get you started with "S.")

Serving describes Jesus' ministry on earth

E_____

R_____

V_____

I_____

C_____

E_____

Write out one thing you liked, learned, or want to do about serving others now that you know Jesus is your friend and shows you how to serve Him.

_____

_____

_____

_____

_____

A Prayer to Pray

Help me, Lord—please! I need Your help right now with making a decision to serve others. I want to begin at home by serving my parents, and even my brothers and sisters. Help me to open my heart, open my eyes, and open my hands and serve as You did. Amen.

6

Jesus Is a Friend Who Understands You

You have probably already discovered that there are many kinds of "friends." For instance, when you go with your parents to another family's home, if there are other kids there, you play together and make new friends. Or if you go with your parents to a home Bible study, you and the other kids there start becoming friends. You have friends at school, even though that may be the only place you see them.

Also you make friends with the kids in the neighborhood as you play together. You can make some friends at your ballet class or in your orchestra or choir. Then you have the friends you make on a soccer, volleyball, basketball, or debate team, or in a science club.

But you also know there are friends who you are "best" friends with. With a best friend, you never run out of things to talk about. Your secret dreams are safe because a best friend won't share them with others. When the two of you are together, it's like you are one person. You think alike and even talk alike and like the same things. She knows just about everything about you—your favorite color, your favorite hobby, your favorite flavor of ice cream—and the list goes on and on.

Well, good news! Your friend Jesus is that kind of friend—and more! He knows you inside and out like nobody else does, and He understands what's going on in your life. He is also there to help you when you are hurting or discouraged or sad or lonely.

As we look at Jesus' life in the Bible, we learn that He had a special ability. When it came to knowing what people needed, He already knew. He didn't have to be told about people's heartaches or problems. It was like He was their closest and best friend. Jesus had the ability to observe and notice when something was missing or not quite right. He knew what people needed, and went into action to meet those needs.

Obviously, we know why Jesus knew all about people— He was God, which means He was omniscient. He knew everything! But Jesus shows *us* what it means to observe a need in other people and do what is necessary to take care of that need. Let's learn from Jesus as He walked among the people of His day.

Fun in God's Word!

In the last chapter we learned about S-E-R-V-I-C-E from the greatest servant of all, our friend Jesus. It was through serving that He met the needs of people. In this chapter we are going to learn more about how Jesus met other people's needs. In one word, taking care of others began with Jesus being **OBSERVANT**.

To be observant means you are aware of your surroundings. If you are familiar with the Nancy Drew mystery books for young women, you know Nancy was a girl detective. She was observant of details, which helped her be aware of what was happening around her. Being observant is also that ability your parents possess when it appears they are reading your mind!

Being observant and understanding is part of Jesus' nature. As God, He notices everything and everybody, and He also knows everything about you. For you and me, being observant is not normal. That's because we are generally selfish. Instead of looking for ways to understand and help others, we focus on ourselves because we tend to think the world revolves around us and our needs.

Looking out for others and their needs is not easy. Therefore, we must make an effort to notice when something is not right with a best friend or someone else around us. Being observant will help you recognize when something is wrong and your friend needs help.

How did Jesus help those around Him?

1. *Jesus healed the sick*. When Jesus was on the earth, there were no hospitals, and there were very few doctors and medicines. Many people who got sick ended up dying because nothing could be done for them. But Jesus knew

and understood when people were sick. In one instance, He stopped at the home of His disciple, Simon Peter:

> As soon as they left the synagogue, they went with James and John to the home of Simon and Andrew. Simon's mother-in-law was in bed with a fever, and they immediately told Jesus about her. So he went to her, took her hand and helped her up. The fever left her and she began to wait on them (Mark 1:29-31).

Who was sick? _____

What did Jesus do? _____

_____

Usually physical illness is easy to see. For instance, your friend comes to school and looks really bad. Maybe she has a serious cough. You understand, like Jesus, that you need to help your friend—take her to the school office or tell your teacher about her need. Like Jesus, as a friend, you are there when someone has a physical problem and you try to help in as many ways as possible.

2. *Jesus had compassion for those who were hurting.* Jesus also noticed those who were sad. Read about what happened one day when Jesus was approaching a city:

> As he approached the town gate, a dead person was being carried out—the only son of his mother, and she was a widow. And a large crowd from the town was with her. When the Lord saw her, his heart went out to her and he said, "Don't

cry." Then he went up and touched the [coffin] they were carrying him on, and the bearers stood still. He said, "Young man, I say to you, get up!" The dead man sat up and began to talk, and Jesus gave him back to his mother (Luke 7:12-15).

How can you tell that Jesus had compassion for the dead son's mother?

_____

_____

_____

Observing others and their needs should result in having compassion. In the scripture above, the Bible says *"his heart went out to her."* That's another way of saying you feel sad for another person. That's what it means to have compassion. You see someone hurting, and you feel sad or bad for them. And if there is anything you can do, your sadness for them turns into action and you do what you can to help.

On another occasion, we read about Jesus' love and care for a 12-year-old girl and her parents in Mark 5:

One of the synagogue leaders, named Jairus, came, and when he saw Jesus, he fell at his feet. He pleaded earnestly with him, "My little daughter is dying. Please come and put your hands on her so that she will be healed and live." So Jesus went with him...While Jesus was still speaking, some people came from the house of Jairus, the synagogue leader. "Your daughter is dead," they said. "Why bother the teacher anymore?"

Overhearing what they said, Jesus told him, "Don't be afraid; just believe."

He did not let anyone follow him except Peter, James and John the brother of James. When they came to the home of the synagogue leader, Jesus saw a commotion, with people crying and wailing loudly. He went in and said to them, "Why all this commotion and wailing? The child is not dead but asleep." But they laughed at him.

After he put them all out, he took the child's father and mother and the disciples who were with him, and went in where the child was. He took her by the hand and said to her, "Talitha koum!" (which means "Little girl, I say to you, get up!") (verses 22-24,35-41).

Make a list of the ways you see Jesus caring about:

The girl's parents _____

_____

_____

_____

The girl _____

_____

_____

_____

_____

For a bonus blessing, read Mark 5:22-34 to get the whole scene and see how Jesus also cared for another woman. What a friend she had in Jesus!

3. *Jesus never refused help to anyone.* With Jesus, there was never any prejudice. Jesus treated everyone the same—after all, every person was His creation in the first place. One time Jesus and His disciples were on a journey and stopped in a place called Samaria. (You can read the full story in John 4.) The Jewish people did not like the Samaritans at all. They avoided the Samaritans and wanted nothing to do with them.

But Jesus did not reject people just because of where they came from. He didn't let the prejudices of others keep Him from talking to the Samaritan woman who came to the local well for water. He cared deeply about all people and was observant and could tell the woman at the well needed help. How did Jesus' disciples react when they saw Him talking to the Samaritan woman?

Just then his disciples returned and were surprised to find him talking with a woman (John 4:27).

Are there any students in your school who are from other countries or from another state or city? Jesus didn't care about where a person was from or that they looked or sounded or dressed differently. Their differences did not keep Jesus from wanting to get to know and help them. Can you think of a student at your school or in your neighborhood who is like this? Write down something you could do next week to try and reach out to even one of these kids.

_____

_____

_____

4. *Jesus loved the unpopular.* It's easy to love people who love you and want to be your friend, or to love those who look, act, and dress like you. But what about those who are not like you? Most kids at school avoid those who are different or unpopular. Sometimes they even make fun of them. They have no desire to understand and help those who are different.

Would Jesus be like this? No. In no way would He avoid or mock those who are different. In another story in the Bible, Jesus met a man named Zacchaeus (see Luke 19:1-10). This man was *the m-o-s-t* unpopular person in town because he was a tax collector. What did Jesus say and want to do when He noticed Zacchaeus sitting in a tree?

> *When Jesus reached the spot, he looked up and said to him, "Zacchaeus, come down immediately. I must stay at your house today." So he came down at once and welcomed him gladly* (Luke 19:5-6).

What did Jesus say and want to do? _____

_____

_____

How did Zacchaeus respond? _____

_____

Now read about how the people around Jesus reacted when they heard He was going to Zacchaeus's home:

All the people saw this and began to mutter, "He has gone to be the guest of a sinner" (Luke 19:7).

_____

_____

Reaching out to those who are unpopular or different is not easy. Yet they need to meet and get to know Jesus just like Zacchaeus did. Jesus is not at your school, but you are. Jesus took notice of you just like He did with Zacchaeus. And you need to take notice of others. When you do that, others might become upset with you, just like some people became upset with Jesus. But you should still try to do as He did. Can you think of someone at school or in your neighborhood or on your ball team you could approach this week and introduce yourself? Write their name here:

_____

5. *Jesus understood spiritual needs.* Jesus had a mission to fulfill when He came to earth. What was that mission, according to Luke 19:10?

The Son of Man came to seek and to save the lost.

_____

_____

According to this next verse, how did Jesus describe lost people?

When he saw the crowds, he had compassion on them, because they were harassed and helpless, like sheep without a shepherd (Matthew 9:36).

_____

_____

What did Jesus tell His disciples was needed to help these people who had no shepherd?

Then he said to his disciples, "The harvest is plentiful but the workers are few. Ask the Lord of the harvest, therefore, to send out workers into his harvest field" (Matthew 9:37-38).

_____

_____

In Matthew 9:37-38, Jesus was telling the disciples that they and others need to be like *"workers"* who harvest crops, and help people who are lost and need to know about Jesus.

What is God's message of love and hope for lost people both then and now, according to John 3:16?

God so loved the world that he gave his one and only Son, that whoever believes in him shall not perish but have eternal life.

Your friend Jesus spent His years of earthly ministry helping people get to know God. He understood their spiritual needs and He cared about them. You can follow in His steps by looking around for those who are hurting and sad. Are there kids you know who are like sheep who have no shepherd? When you form a friendship with these kids, you can introduce them to your friend Jesus—who can help them find eternal life.

What a Friend You Have in Jesus!

Over and over again Jesus observed the needs of others, and He didn't hesitate to take the first step to reach out and help them. Many people came to Jesus for aid, and He was available to them. He even went looking for those who needed His helping hand and His words of encouragement. And guess what? Jesus is looking out for *you* today. He is observing you and sees your needs and is providing for them. How is He doing that?

He has given you parents who take care of you.

He has given you teachers at your church to help care for your spiritual needs.

He has given you your Bible as an instruction book on how to act and what decisions to make. And best of all, as your friend...

He has given you His Spirit to help you act like Him every day of your life.

Again, you have to say, "What a friend I have in Jesus!"

Jesus Is a Friend Who Understands You

In this chapter we had some fun in God's Word as we learned that Jesus was **OBSERVANT**. He paid attention to the needs of others during the whole time He lived on earth, and we should want to follow His example. To help you understand what it means to observe the needs of others, write out the points made in this chapter. I'll get you started with #1.

1. Jesus healed the sick

2. _____

3. _____

4. _____

5. _____

Write out one thing you liked, learned, or want to do after seeing how Jesus cared about others and became their friend.

_____

_____

_____

_____

_____

A Prayer to Pray

Dear Jesus, help me be more friendly to others, to be more aware and caring of those in need. Please give me the love and courage to act and help them with what I can offer. Amen.

7

Jesus Is a Friend Who Is Gracious

esus. Just say His name, and the word *grace* probably comes into your mind. Jesus was the most gracious, giving, generous person who ever lived. Aren't you glad He extended the marvelous gift of His grace and salvation to sinners like you and me?

In our culture today, a gracious person is someone who shows respect, honor, and kindness to others. Not only are they polite, but they are pleasant and courteous. As we look at Jesus, we see that He conducted Himself in gracious behavior at all times while He was on earth.

Jesus showed a gracious and kind attitude to all people. This same kind, respectful attitude is what Jesus wants you to pass on to others as you meet and talk with people in general. And, of course, you want to treat your friends and teachers and other adults with this same courtesy, and especially your parents and family members.

Fun in God's Word!

In this chapter we want to see how Jesus practiced gracious and kind behavior. Because He was perfect, He is a good example to follow. His kind actions show us how to live out His command that we *"be kind...to one another"* (Ephesians 4:32).

Jesus was gracious with His words. Jesus was a teacher, and a teacher must teach. What happened in Jesus' hometown on one occasion, according to Luke 4:16?

He [Jesus] went to Nazareth, where he had been brought up, and on the Sabbath day he went into the synagogue, as was his custom. He stood up to read...

_____

_____

After reading from the Scriptures, Jesus sat down to teach His listeners the meaning of the verses He had read. What was the response of those who had heard Jesus teach (verse 22)?

All spoke well of him and were amazed at the gracious words that came from his lips.

_____

_____

Jesus was known both for His words of kindness and His wisdom. He did not use phony flattery or exaggeration. Today you represent Jesus to those around you. How would you describe your speech toward your family and friends? Here's a list of words that describe how people speak to others.

kindly   respectfully   disrespectfully

uncaring   caring   hurtful

Pick the words that describe how you normally speak to others. You can use each word as many times as needed to describe how you normally speak to...

Friends? _____

Teachers? _____

Other students? _____

Your brothers and sisters? _____

Your parents? _____

If you are honest with yourself, maybe you have come to realize you haven't been as gracious and kind with your words as you should be. That's why this lesson about being kind and gracious should be helpful.

One more thought: A gracious person will say "Please" and "Thank you." Are you a gracious person? If not, what's missing? What changes should you make right away?

I need to _____

_____

I need to stop _____

_____

As a young woman, what do you learn about kindness from God's ideal woman in Proverbs 31:26 (NKJV)?

She opens her mouth with wisdom,
And on her tongue is the law of kindness.

_____

_____

_____

As you read the verse that follows, what rules should you make for your mouth and speech?

Let no corrupt word proceed out of your mouth, but what is good for necessary edification, that it may impart grace to the hearers (Ephesians 4:29 NKJV).

_____

_____

_____

According to the verse that follows, what goal should you have for all your words?

Let your conversation be always full of grace (Colossians 4:6).

_____

_____

Jesus was gracious with people. Have you ever been around someone who made a mistake and another person was happy to point out their mistake in front of others? They maybe even called that person names like "idiot" or "stupid" or "dummy" or worse. Maybe you were the one who received the criticism and name-calling. Hopefully you were not the one doing the name-calling!

Read this story from another time, when Jesus and His 12 disciples were visiting His friends Mary, Martha, and Lazarus (Luke 10:38-42). Martha was upset because her sister Mary was not helping her in the kitchen. Instead, Mary *"sat at the Lord's feet listening to what he said"* (verse 39). Rather than scold Martha or speak harshly to her, Jesus said,

> *Martha, Martha...you are worried and upset about many things, but few things are needed—or indeed only one. Mary has chosen what is better, and it will not be taken away from her* (Luke 10:41-42).

Jesus wanted to gently show Martha that her real priority, her Number One priority—*"what is better"*—was to sit and hear His teaching.

Jesus was sitting right in Martha's house. And she was missing out on knowing, hearing, and worshipping Him! Yet Jesus didn't scold or berate her—He graciously taught her and reminded her that her focus was on her work instead of her worship. What do you want to remember from Jesus' response to Martha the next time someone you are close to makes a mistake or does the wrong thing?

_____

_____

_____

Jesus was kind to people. There is no record in the Bible of Jesus ever refusing anyone who approached Him for help. One wonderful example of how Jesus responded to people appears in Matthew 20:31-34: Two blind beggars called out to Jesus as He was making His way toward Jerusalem during the last week of His life here on earth. How did the crowd treat the blind men?

> *The crowd rebuked them and told them to be quiet, but they shouted all the louder, "Lord, Son of David, have mercy on us!"* (verse 31).

_____

_____

These blind men were told by the crowd to stay quiet, to stop bothering Jesus and quit calling out to Him as He passed by. After all, Jesus was on His way to Jerusalem, and He had important things to take care of. But read the verses that follow, and make a list of what Jesus did.

Jesus stopped and called them. "What do you want me to do for you?" he asked. "Lord," they answered, "we want our sight." Jesus had compassion on them and touched their eyes. Immediately they received their sight and followed him (Matthew 20:32-34).

Jesus _____

Jesus _____

Jesus _____

Do you want to follow Jesus' example and be gracious and show kindness to others? Start by going to your parents and asking them, "How can I help you today?" Then write down how you were able to help. And, of course, you should ask your parents this question every day!

_____

_____

_____

Jesus showed kindness through His touch. When you think of a kind or gracious person, what one act usually shows that person's concern? It's a touch, right? Maybe a hug. A pat on the back. Even a high five. Jesus healed many people. Describe what Jesus did in each of these scenes:

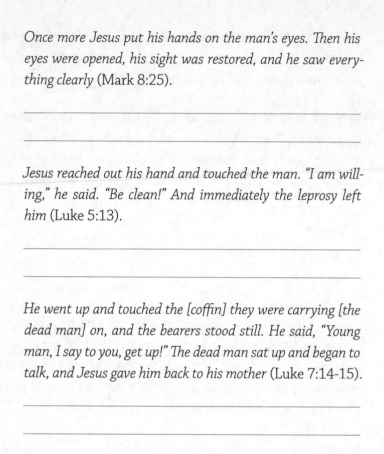

Once more Jesus put his hands on the man's eyes. Then his eyes were opened, his sight was restored, and he saw everything clearly (Mark 8:25).

_____

_____

Jesus reached out his hand and touched the man. "I am willing," he said. "Be clean!" And immediately the leprosy left him (Luke 5:13).

_____

_____

He went up and touched the [coffin] they were carrying [the dead man] on, and the bearers stood still. He said, "Young man, I say to you, get up!" The dead man sat up and began to talk, and Jesus gave him back to his mother (Luke 7:14-15).

_____

_____

The next time a brother or sister or even your mom, dad, or a friend seems to be having a bad day, try following Jesus' example and reach out and touch them. An arm around the waist or shoulders says a lot! You don't even have to say a word. They will know by a simple touch that you care.

Jesus was gracious to outsiders. The Jewish people in Jesus' day were very private and proud of themselves. They didn't want anything to do with people who did not look or act like them. Read on and write out what Jesus did when He met people who were "outsiders" in the eyes of the Jewish nation.

Jesus said to the centurion [a Gentile soldier], "Go! Let it be done just as you believed it would." And his servant was healed at that moment (Matthew 8:13).

_____

_____

The woman was a Greek, born in Syrian Phoenicia. She begged Jesus to drive the demon out of her daughter...Then he told her, "For such a reply, you may go; the demon has left your daughter" (Mark 7:26,29).

_____

_____

In these verses and many more, Jesus was kind and gracious in spite of the fact these people were different and were outsiders to His own group. Write down what you can do this next week when you come in contact with those who are considered "outsiders" by others, even by your friends.

_____

_____

_____

_____

What a Friend You Have in Jesus!

Jesus was perfectly gracious. Because of His love, He was warm, courteous, and kind. He didn't just turn on graciousness when it was needed—and then just as easily turn it off. He didn't act polite only to make a good impression, or because it was expected and required, or to get something He wanted. No, Jesus was gracious in nature, through and through. He was 100 percent genuinely gracious 100 percent of the time to 100 percent of the people He encountered.

And guess what? Jesus is still that warm, kind person who wants to be your friend, and *is* your friend. And He is now asking *you* to have this same attitude—*His* attitude—toward others. You reflect Him when your heart is filled with His love and your mouth speaks with gracious words. The result? People will feel welcome and cared for when they are around you.

And best of all, your graciousness and kindness will draw people to Jesus.

Jesus Is a Friend Who Is Gracious

In this chapter we have had some fun in God's Word. Review again how special your friend Jesus is as you write out the points that show how Jesus was gracious and kind to others.

Jesus was gracious with His words

J _____

J _____

J _____

J _____

Write out one thing you liked, learned, or want to do after discovering that Jesus is a friend who treats people with grace and kindness.

_____

_____

_____

_____

_____

_____

A Prayer to Pray

Gracious Lord, thank You for the wonderful grace You show toward me every single day. You have set a great example for me. Please help me remember to be kind to others and extend Your grace to them. Amen.

8

Jesus Is a Friend Who Is Generous

Do you receive an allowance from your parents, or maybe do chores to earn money? If you do, you probably know how easy it is to spend that money on yourself and how hard it is to give it to others.

Well, your friend Jesus is an awesome model of generosity and unselfishness. To begin the list of what He has so generously given, consider that He gave up His place of honor in heaven to become human. This does not mean He gave up His eternal powers. Rather, it means He chose to live in obedience to the Father's will on earth. *"He became poor"* when He became human because He sacrificed so much (2 Corinthians 8:9).

In fact, Jesus explained that *"foxes have dens and birds have nests, but the Son of Man has no place to lay his head"* (Matthew 8:20). Yet Jesus' sacrifice and generosity in giving up everything, including the comforts of a home, was so that *"you through his poverty might become rich"* through receiving His free gift of salvation and eternal life (2 Corinthians 8:9).

Now that you know this, it's easy to understand that *generosity*, as defined by the life and character of Jesus, means sacrificial giving. Let's look at Jesus' life on this earth to get an idea of how we can follow His actions. But beware! After this study, you may need to turn the level of your generosity way up, even all the way into the range of sacrificing a few things.

Fun in God's Word!

Because Jesus was perfect, His actions show us how to be generous. Each point that follows explains more about being generous and starts with the word GIVING.

Giving was first demonstrated by God the Father. Throughout the Old Testament, from Genesis to Malachi, God is seen as a generous, loving, giving God. For example...

God gave life to Adam and Eve.

God gave safety and salvation to Noah and his family during the Flood.

God gave manna to sustain His chosen people in the wilderness.

God gave the Promised Land to His people for a home.

God gave David the promise of a future king, a Savior who would redeem man from his sin.

God gave His prophets visions of a coming Savior, His very own beloved Son.

God gave His only begotten Son, Jesus.

Giving was modeled by the Son. Without question, Jesus is the ultimate model of giving, for He gave the ultimate gift in the sacrifice of Himself—in death—to forgive our sins and secure eternal life for us. What do you learn about Jesus and what He willingly gave?

> *The Son of Man did not come to be served, but to serve, and to give his life as a ransom for many* (Matthew 20:28).

_____

_____

Giving should be done with the right attitude. In what many call "the Christmas story" in the Bible, the wise men traveled a long distance to bring gifts to the baby Jesus and worship Him. What attitude did the wise men show as they presented their gifts to Jesus, and what kind of generous gifts did they present?

> *On coming to the house, they saw the child with his mother Mary, and they bowed down and worshiped him. Then they opened their treasures and presented him with gifts of gold, frankincense and myrrh* (Matthew 2:11).

_____

_____

Now read 2 Corinthians 9:7 below to learn what the apostle Paul wrote about giving and the kind of heart attitude you should have as you give "gifts" to God.

Each of you should give what you have decided in your heart to give, not reluctantly or under compulsion, for God loves a cheerful giver (2 Corinthians 9:7).

Your giving should not be...

_____

_____

Your giving should be with a _____ heart.

What is God's response to those who give with the right heart attitude?

_____

In the verse that follows, what do you discover about Jesus' attitude as He gave His life as a sacrifice for sin?

For the joy set before him he endured the cross, scorning its shame, and sat down at the right hand of the throne of God (Hebrews 12:2).

_____

Jesus willingly, joyfully gave Himself as a sacrifice for sin—your sin. Take a minute to review the verses in this section—"Giving should be with the right attitude."

Knowing that God loves a cheerful giver, what should be your attitude when it is time to give back to God?

_____

_____

_____

Giving has nothing to do with how much you have. Jesus pointed out this truth through the actions of an amazing woman. Read her story below:

Jesus sat down opposite the place where the offerings were put and watched the crowd putting their money into the temple treasury. Many rich people threw in large amounts. But a poor widow came and put in two very small copper coins, worth only a few cents.

Calling his disciples to him, Jesus said, "Truly I tell you, this poor widow has put more into the treasury than all the others. They all gave out of their wealth; but she, out of her poverty, put in everything—all she had to live on" (Mark 12:41-44).

How much money did the rich people give?

_____

How much money did the poor widow give?

_____

Who gave the most, the rich people or the widow, and why?

_____

_____

Jesus explained that the widow gave more than all the others. How was that possible? Because the others *"gave out of their wealth"* at little personal cost and sacrifice, while the widow gave *"out of her poverty."* In comparison, she had given the most—she gave *all* that she had to live on!

Jesus also gave all that He had—His life. What one thing can you do this week to follow the example set by Jesus and the widow? (This would be a good thing to talk over with your parents.)

_____

_____

Remember, it's not *what you have* that's important, but *what you are willing to give* that's important to God!

Giving shows where your heart is. Giving is a matter of the heart. The Pharisees, a group of religious leaders in Jesus' day, made a great show of giving to the poor. However, Jesus taught that people should do just the opposite when they gave generously. In one word, how did Jesus say giving should be done according to Matthew 6:3-4?

When you give to the needy, do not let your left hand know what your right hand is doing, so that your giving may be in secret.

Giving God's way shows what is really in your heart because you are giving to God and making sure no one else knows what you are giving. What result is mentioned in verse 4?

Then your Father, who sees what is done in secret, will reward you.

Giving provides a savings account in heaven. You probably have a piggy bank—maybe more than one! Parents and grandparents love to give piggy banks to their children and grandchildren, hoping each child will learn to save some money. Saving is a good life discipline to learn and establish as a habit. But Jesus has a warning and some instructions regarding your heart and what you do with the money you have and save. In His famous Sermon on the Mount, Jesus described how earthly treasures can easily be lost (Matthew 6:19-21).

Do not store up for yourselves treasures on earth, where moths and vermin destroy, and where thieves break in and steal. But store up for yourselves treasures in heaven, where moths and vermin do not destroy, and where thieves do not break in and steal. For where your treasure is, there your heart will be also.

What is Jesus' warning, and why?

_____

_____

_____

What does Jesus say to do instead, and why?

_____

_____

_____

Jesus then states a truth: *"For where your treasure is, there your heart will be also"* (verse 21). When it comes to giving, what do you think Jesus meant by this statement?

_____

_____

_____

Verse 21 is a key principle to remember and memorize. It points out that whatever occupies your thoughts and time is where your affections—your heart—will be.

Giving isn't always about money. Jesus told a story about a man who was robbed and beaten while on a journey. (You can read the full story in Luke 10:29-36.) Two people who walked by the wounded man did not stop to help him, but the third man who came by stopped. What did the third man do for the wounded man?

He went to him and bandaged his wounds, pouring on oil and wine. Then he put the man on his own donkey, brought him to an inn and took care of him (verse 3).

_____

_____

_____

_____

You may not have much money to give to the needs of others right now, but you can be a giver by offering a helping hand—to your mom and dad and brothers and sisters around the house, or to a friend who is having a hard time. It will only cost you your time—but what a gift!

What a Friend You Have in Jesus!

Can you imagine having everything and yet being willing to give it all up? That's exactly what Jesus did, which proves how much your friend Jesus loves you: *"Greater love* has no one than this: to lay down one's life for one's friends" (John 15:13). If you want to be like Jesus, then giving is a must. No one can out-give God, but if you are Jesus' friend, you should want to follow His example and give to God's work and for the needs of others. As Jesus told His disciples and now is telling you, *Freely you have received; freely give* " (Matthew 10:8).

A good place to start giving is at home. At your age you might not have much money, but there are other ways you can give. For example, you can give the gift of obedience to your parents. Each day, see yourself as offering up your life, or giving your all to serve Jesus, by doing what your parents want you to do and helping them when you see a need or an opportunity. Being willing to give isn't really optional. In fact, God commands it—and adds the bonus of a promise and a blessing when you do:

Children, obey your parents in the Lord, for this is right. "Honor your father and mother"—which is the first commandment with a promise—"so that it may go well with you and that you may enjoy long life on the earth" (Ephesians 6:1-3).

Do as God asks—obey your parents. Honor them. Love them. Serve them. Help them. Pray for them. Appreciate them. Do it with the right attitude, which is your choice, and you will be blessed. And don't forget to be a giver to your brothers and sisters. Everyone needs some help and encouragement.

Jesus Is a Friend Who Is Generous

In this chapter we have had some fun in God's Word. Review again how special your friend Jesus is as you write out the points that show you how generous He was to others. Here's an example:

*g*iving was first demonstrated by God the Father

g _____

g _____

g _____

g _____

g _____

g _____

Write out one thing you liked, learned, or want to do after discovering that Jesus is a friend who is generous.

_____

_____

_____

_____

A Prayer to Pray

Lord Jesus, I am amazed that You gave the most costly gift of all when You sacrificed Yourself to pay for my sins. Wow. I want to thank You with all my heart! I want to become a generous giver like You. Please help me start right in my own home with my family. Amen.

9

Jesus Is a Friend Who Is Faithful

You probably won't meet very many people who are truly faithful. Something in us wants to be lazy, do it later, wait a little longer, or take a shortcut. But this was not so with Jesus!

Jesus was faithful to God's purpose. He came to earth for a purpose, declaring, *"My food...is to do the will of him who sent me and to finish his work"* (John 4:34). Jesus' work was to live and die as the perfect sacrifice for man's sin.

But as Jesus *"went around doing good"* (Acts 10:38) and feeding the multitudes who followed Him, His followers grew into a multitude of thousands. The people had a different purpose in mind for Jesus, especially after they witnessed Him feeding 5000-plus men and probably also their families. They wanted Jesus to be their leader and to provide food for them on a regular basis. (You can read the full story in John 6:22-33.)

But despite many distractions and the desires and demands of the people, Jesus was faithful to God's plan and told the crowds, *"I have come down from heaven not to do my will but to do the will of him who sent me"* (John 6:38).

Fun in God's Word!

Faithfully following Jesus will require you to ask the question, "Am I willing to listen to Jesus and not to 'them'—not to listen to the voices of my friends, to other students at school or kids in my neighborhood, to the popular people, to TV, magazines, and the words in music?"

If you haven't already made a commitment to be loyal to Jesus, it's time. You can do this by saying in your heart, "Jesus, I am willing to follow in Your steps and be faithful regardless of what others may say or do to me."

To help you with your commitment to being faithful, we will use the word **FAITHFULNESS** in this chapter to show how your friend Jesus was faithful in all things.

Faithfulness starts with God, the Father. The Bible speaks of God's faithfulness. Write out what each of these verses says about God's faithfulness.

Because of the LORD's great love we are not consumed, for his compassions never fail. They are new every morning; great is your faithfulness (Lamentations 3:22-23).

_____

_____

Great is your love, reaching to the heavens; your faithfulness reaches to the skies (Psalm 57:10).

_____

_____

Here are a few more verses in which God showed Himself to be faithful:

He was faithful to provide coverings for Adam and Eve after their disobedience (Genesis 3:21).

He was faithful to promise a Savior (Genesis 3:15).

He was faithful to fulfill His promise that Jesus, God's only Son, would be born as Savior (Luke 2:11).

He was faithful to give the world a divine model of His very nature through the life and ministry of Jesus as He walked among us as God in human flesh (John 1:14).

Faithfulness is modeled by the Son. To the very end of His life, day by day Jesus faithfully moved toward the purpose God set for Him. On the night before His death, Jesus declared His faithfulness to the Father. How faithful was Jesus in completing His mission? Or, put another way, what did Jesus do that revealed His faithfulness to God and to fulfilling His will?

I have brought you glory on earth by finishing the work you gave me to do (John 17:4).

_____

What tasks have your parents asked of you this week? Write them here:

_____

_____

_____

_____

Now check the ones to which you can say, "I have finished the work that was given to me."

Faithfulness was seen in Jesus' prayers. Jesus was also faithful in prayer. One of the most amazing things about Jesus coming to earth as a man was the fact that He chose to submit Himself to the control of the Holy Spirit. Prayer was a key way Jesus communicated with the Father and received His Father's direction. After a very busy and strenuous day, what did Jesus do?

Very early in the morning, while it was still dark, Jesus got up, left the house and went off to a solitary place, where he prayed (Mark 1:35).

_____

What did Jesus do when He had a big decision to make about His ministry?

Jesus went out to a mountainside to pray, and spent the night praying to God. When morning came, he called his disciples to him and chose twelve of them (Luke 6:12-13).

_____

What did Jesus do when He was concerned that His disciples were under spiritual attack from Satan?

Simon, Simon, Satan has asked to sift all of you as wheat. But I have prayed for you, Simon, that your faith may not fail (Luke 22:31-32).

_____

What is Jesus doing right now in heaven?

Christ Jesus...is at the right hand of God and is also interceding [praying] for us (Romans 8:34).

_____

Jesus was faithful to pray when He was on earth, and even now while He is in heaven He is faithfully praying for you (Hebrews 7:25). What do the verses above and Jesus' example of faithful prayer teach you about being faithful to pray?

_____

_____

_____

Faithfulness is a sign of devotion. Can you imagine what Jesus' last day was like? It was the most horrible day ever on earth. Yet a loyal band of women who often traveled with Jesus and supported Him in many ways were present with Jesus the day of His crucifixion and death. These women were seen at the foot of the cross—faithful to the end—while Jesus' own disciples could not handle the scene and all fled, except for John. What do you see the faithful band of women doing on the third day after Jesus' death?

When the Sabbath was over, [the women] bought spices so that they might go to anoint Jesus' body. Very early on the first day of the week, just after sunrise, they were on their way to the tomb (Mark 16:1-2).

_____

_____

Even though these women had witnessed a great tragedy and were in grave danger as they mourned the loss of a friend, they were faithful to their friend Jesus to the end, bringing spices to properly prepare Jesus' body for burial.

How does the faithful devotion of these women encourage you to be faithful in your devotion to Jesus?

_____

_____

_____

Can you think of something—a task or project or assignment or upcoming event—you have not taken care of or are putting off? Jot it down here—and do it!

_____

_____

Faithfulness was part of Jesus' ministry to His disciples. Jesus was faithful to protect His disciples while He was physically with them. In your own words, what did Jesus tell the Father in prayer on the night before His death?

None has been lost except the one doomed to destruction [Judas] so that Scripture would be fulfilled (John 17:12).

_____

_____

Jesus' promise to protect His disciples continues on for you and all who put their faith and trust in Him. Underline each promise Jesus made in John 10:28-29 about keeping you safe:

I give them eternal life, and they shall never perish; no one will snatch them out of my hand.

My Father, who has given them to me, is greater than all; no one can snatch them out of my Father's hand.

Take a moment to stop what you are doing and offer up a silent prayer to thank Jesus for His faithfulness—for faithfully keeping watch over you.

Faithfulness begins with family. Jesus was faithful to His family, and so should you be faithful to your family. What does this verse tell you about Jesus' commitment to His family when He was 12 years old?

He went down to Nazareth with them [His parents] and was obedient to them (Luke 2:51).

Even at the end of His life, Jesus was faithful to respect and watch over Mary, His mother. Looking down from the cross upon His mother and His disciple John, He asked John to take care of Mary. In a few words, what did John do according to John 19:26-27?

When Jesus saw his mother there, and the disciple whom he loved [John] standing nearby, he said to her, "Woman, here is your son," and to the disciple, "Here is your mother." From that time on, this disciple took her into his home.

Obeying your parents is an act of faithfulness. In fact, it is a command from the Lord—*"Children, obey your parents in the Lord, for this is right"* (Ephesians 6:1).

What a Friend You Have in Jesus!

As a young woman who is a Christian, it is vital that faithfulness be a quality that describes you and shines brightly in your life. When you are faithful, you show that you are born of God and belong to Him through His Son. Jesus was committed to faithfully doing and fulfilling the Father's will. He was also faithful to His disciples and His family and others. He also faithfully prayed for them. And now, as you have seen in this book, Jesus is faithfully praying for *you* and caring for *you*, His friend.

As you walk in faithfulness, you mirror the heart of your steadfast Savior. You also bear fruit that shows Christ lives in you. Your whole family is blessed when they can depend on you and trust you.

In this chapter we have looked at many instances of Jesus' faithfulness. And the good news is you can develop the same faithfulness Jesus showed the world. You can grow in faithfulness that follows through, fulfills your responsibilities, shows up, and keeps your word and your commitments.

If this sounds impossible or like a hard uphill climb, take Step One: Call upon God in prayer. Then start small—in the little things. And count on Jesus' strength. In Him you can do all things, including being faithful (Philippians 4:13). Also ask God to help you get rid of laziness and fulfill this major purpose He has for you—that you would be *"faithful in all things"* (1 Timothy 3:11 NKJV).

Jesus Is a Friend Who Is Faithful

In this chapter we have had some fun in God's Word. Review again how special your friend Jesus is as you write out the points that show us about Jesus' **FAITHFULNESS**.

$\mathcal{F}$aithfulness starts with God, the Father

$\mathcal{F}$_____

$\mathcal{F}$_____

$\mathcal{F}$_____

$\mathcal{F}$_____

$\mathcal{F}$_____

Write out one thing you liked, learned, or want to do after discovering that Jesus is a friend who is faithful.

_____

_____

_____

A Prayer to Pray

Lord Jesus, help me day by day to be faithful like You are. I want to do what I say I will do. I want to be a young woman who keeps my word. I want to finish what I start, beginning at home with my family and with my friends. Amen.

10

Jesus Is a Friend Who Is Wise

When I became a Christian, a woman suggested that I should read one chapter of Proverbs every day—the chapter that matched the day's date. She explained, "For instance, if the date is the first day of the month, you read Proverbs 1. If the date is the tenth day of the month, you read Proverbs 10."

Then she asked, "Do you get it?"

And I replied, "Yes, whatever the date is, I am supposed to read the chapter in Proverbs that is the same number as the date."

Well, I got it, and I'm so glad I did! And I hope you are getting it too. Every single sentence and verse in the book of Proverbs is 100 percent pure wisdom and very clearly tells you what to do and what not to do. That is the purpose of the book of Proverbs, as Solomon wrote in Proverbs 1, beginning at verse 1:

1 *The proverbs of Solomon son of David, king of Israel:*

2 for gaining wisdom and instruction;
   for understanding words of insight;
3 for receiving instruction in prudent behavior,
   doing what is right and just and fair;
4 for giving prudence to those who are simple,
   knowledge and discretion to the young—
5 let the wise listen and add to their learning,
   and let the discerning get guidance...
32 For the waywardness of the simple will kill them,
   and the complacency of fools will destroy them;
33 but whoever listens to me will live in safety
   and be at ease, without fear of harm.

Of all the qualities we have studied in this book, wisdom has to be one of the most important qualities to look for in a friend. Why? Well, I don't know about you, but most of my friends make as many mistakes as I do. So, it's nice to have a friend like Jesus to show us the way and help us learn how to make better choices.

Jesus definitely shows us the way. His entire life is a study of wisdom, and He is the perfect example of it. Who better to teach us about wisdom than Jesus, the wisest person who ever lived? In fact, Jesus *is* wisdom. As God, He had perfect knowledge. Therefore, He acted in perfect wisdom. And when Jesus was on earth, He made all the right choices. What is wisdom? It is seen in...

the choices you make,

the actions you take, and

the words you speak.

All summed up, wisdom is the correct application of knowledge. A good goal for you is to learn how to find and develop the wisdom you need, the wisdom that makes you more like Jesus—in the way you live and the decisions you make.

Fun in God's Word!

How can you develop wisdom? Or, put another way, how can you be more like Jesus and make right decisions more often? To answer these questions, let's look again at the life of Jesus, and especially His wise actions. Let's look at five facts that will help you understand the importance of getting WISDOM.

Wisdom's starting point is Jesus. From the beginning of this book, we've been talking about being more like your friend Jesus—and that's exactly where true wisdom begins. From the minute you accept Jesus as your Savior and friend, you take on a new life, Jesus' life. That's what Nicodemus, a teacher in Israel, learned. He came to Jesus wanting to find out more about Him. What did Jesus tell Nicodumus he must do when he came seeking truth and wisdom?

Jesus replied, "Very truly I tell you, no one can see the kingdom of God unless they are born again" (John 3:3).

What was true of Nicodemus applies to you as well: You must be born again. You must start over with Jesus in your life. Being "born again" means you truly know the God of all wisdom—Jesus.

What two changes occur in your life when you accept Christ as your Savior and are born again as a "new creation"?

If anyone is in Christ, the new creation has come: The old has gone, the new is here! (2 Corinthians 5:17).

Change #1 _____

_____

Change #2 _____

_____

Wisdom's teacher is the Holy Spirit. When Jesus was on earth, His every action was done with wisdom. He also taught wisdom to the people who heard Him speak. He was *the* source of wisdom while on this earth. When Jesus began talking about dying and leaving His disciples, they became very concerned. What did Jesus say He would do so the disciples would not be without His wisdom after He went back to heaven?

When the Advocate comes, whom I will send to you from the Father—the Spirit of truth who goes out from the Father— he will testify about me (John 15:26).

_____

What was *"the Advocate"*—the one who will testify about Jesus—called?

_____

According to the verses that follow, what is the Holy Spirit's role in the life of a believer?

When he, the Spirit of truth, comes, he will guide you into all the truth (John 16:13).

The Holy Spirit will _____

_____

We continually ask God to fill you with the knowledge of his will through all the wisdom and understanding that the Spirit gives (Colossians 1:9).

The Holy Spirit will give you _____

_____

Wisdom's handbook is the Bible. The path to true wisdom begins when Jesus becomes your personal Savior and friend. That's also when the power and guidance and wisdom of the Holy Spirit becomes available to you. But that's not all you need for a life of making right choices. You need the wisdom of Jesus that comes from knowing His Word, the Bible.

What did the psalmist say happens when you read and think about the teachings the Bible gives you?

Oh, how I love your law [the Bible]! I meditate on it all day long. Your commands are always with me and make me wiser than my enemies (Psalm 119:97-98).

Your commands _____

_____

Your commands _____

_____

Getting to know Jesus by reading your Bible will give you the knowledge you need to make wise decisions, better choices, and speak with wisdom. Jesus has an exciting plan for your life. As you read your Bible, you grow in wisdom, which prepares you for Jesus' purpose for you.

Wisdom's path requires prayer. It's hard to believe, but Jesus, who was God in human flesh, constantly looked to the Father for wisdom through prayer. What do you see Jesus doing in the Garden of Gethsemane as He prepared to make His way to the cross?

He fell with his face to the ground and prayed..."*may your will be done*" (Matthew 26:39,42).

_____

_____

Read the instructions Jesus gave about praying in Matthew 7:7. A good way to remember Jesus' instructions is to think of **A-S-K**:

Ask and it will be given to you;

Seek and you will find;

Knock and the door will be opened to you (Matthew 7:7).

What is the result of **A-S-K**ing, according to verse 8?

For everyone who asks receives; the one who seeks finds; and to the one who knocks, the door will be opened.

Those who ask— _____

Those who seek— _____

Those who knock— _____

Read the advice James 1:5 gives about getting wisdom:

If any of you lacks wisdom, you should ask God, who gives generously to all without finding fault, and it will be given to you.

When should you ask for wisdom?

_____

Whom should you ask for wisdom?

_____

How is God described?

_____

_____

What is the promise and the result of asking for wisdom?

_____

Wisdom is available to you when you pray—when you A-S-K. Whatever happens in your crazy or bad day, ask God for help. Whenever you need to make a decision, stop for a minute and check in with God. A-S-K Him for His help—for His wisdom.

Wisdom's progress is ongoing. Jesus was wisdom in a man's body. He was God. But He chose to allow Himself to progress like other kids while growing up. What does this verse say about Jesus' normal human growth progress—about the four areas in which He grew?

Jesus grew in wisdom and stature, and in favor with God and man (Luke 2:52).

Jesus grew in _____

Jesus grew in _____

Jesus grew in _____

Jesus grew in _____

Jesus grew physically, mentally, spiritually, socially, and in wisdom. And you need to do the same and go through the same growth process Jesus did. Wisdom does not come overnight. But the good news is that you can speed up your progress by setting a goal to *"get wisdom."* As Proverbs 4:7 instructs,

The beginning of wisdom is this: Get wisdom.
Though it cost all you have, get understanding.

How can you make this happen? These verses from the book of Proverbs tell you how it's done. As you read the proverbs below, underline the actions you see that will help you grow and progress in wisdom as modeled by Jesus.

The Reward of Wisdom

Blessed are those who find wisdom, those who gain understanding, for she is more profitable than silver and yields better returns than gold (Proverbs 3:13-14).

The Source of Wisdom

The fear of the LORD is the beginning of wisdom (Proverbs 9:10).

The Effort of Finding Wisdom

If you look for [wisdom] as for silver and search for it as for hidden treasure, then you will understand the fear of the LORD and find the knowledge of God (Proverbs 2:4-5).

The Importance of Trusting God's Wisdom

Trust in the LORD with all your heart and lean not on your own understanding; in all your ways submit to him, and he will make your paths straight (Proverbs 3:5-6).

What a Friend You Have in Jesus!

Isn't it great to have a friend like Jesus who is always available to you? Jesus always knows the right thing to do, and He lets you know the right thing to do whenever you seek His advice and **A-S-K** Him for wisdom.

Because Jesus was perfect, He made perfect decisions and choices. Sadly, this will not always be true of you. You probably already know that when you try and do things your own way...well, it's not pretty! But when you choose to turn to Jesus and seek His advice by reading your Bible, praying for help, and asking your parents, you will find the wisdom you need. You will know it is wisdom because:

You will start seeing life from God's point of view.

You will begin choosing better courses of action.

You will be happy with the results of the wisdom you are applying—and so will the other people in your life.

You will make fewer mistakes and goofs, both in your behavior and in your choices. And most important of all...

You will be acting more and more like your friend Jesus.

Jesus Is a Friend Who Is Wise

In this chapter we have had some fun in God's Word. Review again how special your friend Jesus is as you write out the points that show you how to follow Jesus down the path of **WISDOM**. (I'll get you started with the first point.)

Wisdom's starting point is <u>Jesus</u>

Wisdom's teacher is _____

Wisdom's handbook is _____

Wisdom's path requires _____

Wisdom's progress is _____

Write out one thing you liked, learned, or want to do about growing more wise—just like Jesus.

_____

_____

_____

_____

A Prayer to Pray

Lord Jesus, thank You for setting a pattern for me to follow as You grew in wisdom, walked in wisdom, spoke with wisdom, and lived out wisdom. I'm so glad You show me and teach me how to be more wise. Help me to always **A-S-K** You for wisdom as I make choices. I really need it! Amen.

Bestselling Books for Girls by Elizabeth George

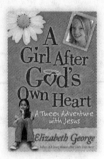

A Girl After God's Own Heart

Homework! Friends! Activities! Parents! The life of a tween girl is full of so much action—and sometimes so much *confusion!* How can I find a real best friend? How can I get along with my brothers and sisters? How can I make time in my busy life for Jesus? How can I know the right things to say and do—especially when I keep messing up? As you set out on this fun adventure with Jesus, you'll learn what it means to be a girl after God's own heart. Start today!

A Girl's Guide to Discovering Her Bible

The Bible is God's message especially for you. In it, you will find out what He wants you to know—about getting along with your family, finding good friends, how to do well in your schoolwork, and more. The Bible is the most incredible book you will ever read. Discover what it says, and how it can help you every single day.

A Girl's Guide to Making Really Good Choices

Have you ever counted how many choices you make each day? A lot! What should I say...or not say? How should I spend my time right now? When will I do my schoolwork? My chores? Who should I choose as my friends? What should I wear...eat...watch...read?

God says that when you make good choices, your day will go so much better. So start now, and learn how to make the best kinds of choices!

A Girl After God's Own Heart Devotional

Wouldn't you love to get advice from Someone who cares about everything you're going through? You can! God wants to help you through good days and bad, encourage your hopes and dreams, and guide your thoughts and feelings. Get ready to listen to the heart of God and discover how much He loves you!

Bestselling Books for Teen Girls
by Elizabeth George

A Young Woman After God's Own Heart

What does it mean to include God's heart in your everyday life? It means understanding and following His perfect plan for your friendships, your faith, your family relationships, and your future. Learn how to grow close to God, enjoy meaningful relationships, make wise choices, become spiritually strong, build a better future, and fulfill the desires of your heart.

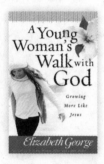

A Young Woman's Walk with God

Love, joy, peace, patience, kindness, goodness, faithfulness, gentleness, and self-control are qualities Jesus possessed—and He wants you to have them too. Elizabeth George takes you step-by-step through the fruit of the Spirit to help you get the most out of your life.

A Young Woman's Guide to Discovering Her Bible

What does God have to say about the issues nearest to your heart? Things like acceptance, loneliness, friendships? You'll discover all that and much more when you make God's Word your personal guide in all you do. Learn how to get the most out of your Bible, which will draw you closer to God and ignite exciting changes in your life!

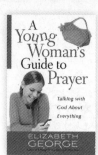

A Young Woman's Guide to Prayer

God has given you an amazing gift—the ability to talk with Him every day. Through prayer, you can share with God your joys and triumphs, hurts and fears, wants and needs. He cares about every detail of your life. God is your forever friend, and He's always ready to talk with you!

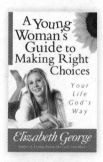

A Young Woman's Guide to Making Right Choices

When it comes to making decisions, how can you make sure you are making the right choices, the best choices? Do you desire to please God in the way you pick your friends, spend your time, and treat your family? You'll find useful checkpoints for helping you understand God's wisdom and living it out.

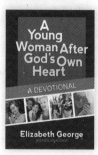

A Young Woman After God's Own Heart—A Devotional

God wants to encourage you each and every day. He has things to say to you that can change your day, take away your worries, and give you hope. In His amazing love, He cares about all the details of your life. In this pocket-sized devotional, you'll learn how to take your problems to God, let go of your worries, live your faith, find a real friend in Jesus, and grow in true beauty and confidence.

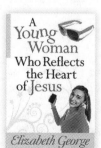

A Young Woman Who Reflects the Heart of Jesus

As you grow up, life gets more exciting, more fun... and more challenging. So much more to do, so many more choices to make. How can you consistently do what is best—and avoid making bad mistakes—at every step of the way? Jesus is the perfect example for how to handle life. From Him you'll learn 12 character qualities that can make every area of your life better!

To learn more about Harvest House books and
to read sample chapters, visit our website:

www.harvesthousepublishers.com

HARVEST HOUSE PUBLISHERS
EUGENE, OREGON